The Story of
Eleanor Roosevelt

by Rachel A. Koestler-Grack

CHELSEA
CLUBHOUSE
An Imprint of Chelsea House Publishers
A Haights Cross Communications Company
Philadelphia

Chelsea Clubhouse books are published by Chelsea House Publishers, a subsidiary of Haights Cross Communications

A Haights Cross Communications ✦ Company

The Chelsea House World Wide Web address is www.chelseahouse.com

Printed and bound in the United States of America.
9 8 7 6 5 4 3 2 1

Library of Congress Cataloging-in-Publication Data
Koestler-Grack, Rachel A., 1973–
The story of Eleanor Roosevelt / by Rachel A. Koestler-Grack.
    p. cm. — (Breakthrough biographies)
Summary: Chronicles the life of Eleanor Roosevelt, from her privileged childhood to her accomplishments as First Lady of the United States, to her work with the United Nations.
Includes bibliographical references and index.
    ISBN 0-7910-7313-0
1. Roosevelt, Eleanor, 1884–1962— Juvenile literature. 2. Presidents' spouses— United States— Biography— Juvenile literature. [1. Roosevelt, Eleanor, 1884–1962. 2. First ladies. 3. Women— Biography] I. Title. II. Series.
    E807.1.R48K64 2004
    973.917'092— dc21   2003000269

Selected Sources

Collier, Peter with David Horowitz. *The Roosevelts: An American Saga.* New York: Simon & Schuster, 1994.

Freedman, Russell. *Eleanor Roosevelt: A Life of Discovery.* New York: Clarion Books, 1993.

Lash, Joseph P. *"Life Was Meant to Be Lived": A Centenary Portrait of Eleanor Roosevelt.* New York: W.W. Norton, 1984.

Roosevelt, Eleanor. *The Autobiography of Eleanor Roosevelt.* New York: Harper, 1961.

Editorial Credits

Colleen Sexton, editor; Takeshi Takahashi, designer; Mary Englar, photo researcher; Jennifer Krassy Peiler, layout

Content Reviewer

Allida Black, Ph.D., Project Director, The Eleanor Roosevelt Papers, The George Washington University, Washington, D.C.

Photo Credits

Hulton Archive/Getty Images: cover; AP/Wide World: title page, 23, 24 (bottom); Franklin D. Roosevelt Library: 4, 5, 6, 7 (both), 8, 10, 11 (both), 12, 13, 14, 15, 17, 18, 26, 27 (bottom); Bettmann/Corbis: 9, 16, 20, 27 (top), 29 (Mary A. Hallaren); Corbis: 19, 21, 25 (right), 29 (Jeannette Rankin); Stock Montage, Inc.: 22, 24 (top); Hulton-Deutcsch Collection/Corbis: 25 (left); New York Public Library: 29 (Marian Anderson); Library of Congress: 29 (Amelia Earhart); Rondal and Elizabeth W. Partridge: 29 (Dorothea Lange); Rick Apitz: back cover.

Table of Contents

A Long Night

Most residents of Paris, France, were asleep in the early morning hours of December 10, 1948. But members of the **United Nations** were wide awake and had much to do. They had come to Paris from all over the world to vote on a Universal Declaration of Human Rights. Eleanor Roosevelt, a **delegate** from the United States, had led the group that wrote the declaration.

Eleanor was a **humanitarian**. She believed all people are equal and deserve the same basic freedoms, no matter where in the world they live. She thought everyone should have the right to get an education, to be paid for a job, and to practice the religion they choose. Eleanor had worked hard on the Universal Declaration of Human Rights. For two years, she settled arguments among delegates with opposing views. Every nation had wanted the declaration worded just right. Now they awaited the vote.

Eleanor Roosevelt holds a copy of the Universal Declaration of Human Rights, one of her greatest accomplishments. The document has been printed in the languages of every country. It lists the rights that belong to all people in the world.

Eleanor traveled all over the world in her work with the United Nations. Here, she is greeted by children in Israel in 1952.

At 3:00 in the morning, the United Nations approved the declaration. No country voted against it. Then the delegates rose to their feet to honor Eleanor with a standing ovation. This had never before happened at the United Nations. Eleanor's leadership had inspired the delegates. And the Declaration of Human Rights inspired the world. Some people called it the best document ever created by the United Nations.

Eleanor was 63 years old when the United Nations passed the declaration. But this event was only the latest in a lifetime of great accomplishments. She had worked as a teacher, a writer, and a speaker. She had fought for the rights of women and blacks. And she had helped the poor and the sick around the world. As First Lady of the United States, she made people feel they had a caring government. Eleanor told everyone, "Life has got to be lived—that's all there is to it." And what a full life she led.

> *"Where, after all, do universal human rights begin? In small places, close to home. So close and so small that they cannot be seen on any maps of the world."*
> —Eleanor Roosevelt

An Awkward Girl

Anna Eleanor Roosevelt was born on October 11, 1884, into a wealthy and well-respected family. Her father was Elliott Roosevelt, the brother of future president Theodore Roosevelt. Her mother was Anna Hall, who was a noted beauty. Eleanor and her family lived in New York City.

A shy girl, Eleanor had an awkward walk and teeth that stuck out. Her mother believed that beauty and good manners were important. She was ashamed of Eleanor's looks and made her feel bad.

Eleanor, here at age 3, remembered herself as "a solemn child, without beauty and painfully shy." But her father called her "a miracle from heaven."

Eleanor was close to her father. He showed her a great deal of love. "With my father I was perfectly happy," she later remembered. "He was the center of my world and all around him loved him." Elliott called Eleanor "Little Nell" after a character in one of her favorite books, *The Old Curiosity Shop* by Charles Dickens. Eleanor liked this name much better than "Granny," the name her mother called her.

Eleanor's mother, Anna Hall Roosevelt, came from a wealthy and well-known family. Her ancestors signed the Declaration of Independence in 1776.

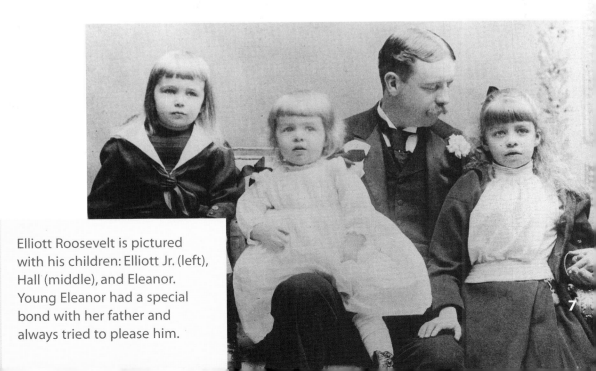

Elliott Roosevelt is pictured with his children: Elliott Jr. (left), Hall (middle), and Eleanor. Young Eleanor had a special bond with her father and always tried to please him.

July 10th 1894

Dear Father
I hope you are well. I am now in Bar-Harbor and am having a lovely time yester day I went to the Indian encampm to see some pretty things I have to fin out the paths all a lone I walked up to the top of Kebo mountain this morn-ing and I walk three hours every afternoon. Brudie walks from 4 to 5 miles every day. Please write to me soon. We eat our meals at the hotel and the names of the things we get to eat ar to funny Washington pie an deal are mild to some other things we get. I have lessons every day with Grandma. With a great deal of love I a your little daughter. Nell.

While Eleanor's father was away, she wrote letters to him regularly.

When Eleanor was 7 years old, her family started to fall apart. Her father was an **alcoholic**. He moved to a farm in Virginia to work at getting better. Eleanor and her two younger brothers, Elliott Jr. and Hall, stayed in New York with their mother. Eleanor missed her father very much. She couldn't understand why he had to be away from his family.

Just before Eleanor's eighth birthday, her mother became sick with the disease diphtheria. Anna died on December 7, 1892, and Elliott hurried home from Virginia. Eleanor didn't grieve much for her mother. She later wrote, "Death meant nothing to me, and one fact wiped out everything else. My father was back and I would see him soon."

When Eleanor saw her father again, he was full of grief over Anna's death. She later remembered, "He was dressed all in black, looking very sad. He held out his arms and gathered me to him." Elliott told Eleanor that she and her brothers were all he had left in the world. But before she died, Anna had asked that the children live with their Grandmother Hall. Elliott followed her wishes.

> "To handle yourself, use your head; to handle others, use your heart."
>
> —Eleanor Roosevelt

Almost two years later, Eleanor's father died after a fall. When her aunts told her the news, Eleanor was overcome with grief. She knew she would always keep memories of her father close to her heart.

Eleanor spent summers at Oak Terrace, her Grandmother Hall's country house. She loved the outdoors and enjoyed riding and jumping her pony.

Anna Roosevelt had wanted her daughter to be educated in Europe. Grandmother Hall finally agreed in 1899 to send Eleanor to Allenswood, a girls' school near London, England. At age 15, Eleanor joined 34 other girls who would be guided by Mademoiselle Marie Souvestre, the school's headmistress.

Mademoiselle Souvestre took a deep interest in Eleanor. She thought Eleanor was smart, kind-hearted, and a born leader. Eleanor almost always sat across from Mademoiselle Souvestre

"No one can make you feel inferior without your consent."

—Eleanor Roosevelt

During vacations from school, Eleanor became Mademoiselle Souvestre's traveling companion. Eleanor called their trips to France and Italy "one of the most momentous things that happened in my education."

10

during meals. Only the best students received this honor. Some evenings, the headmistress discussed **politics** with the girls in her study. She also read them poetry and stories. "Mlle. Souvestre shocked me into thinking, and that on the whole was very beneficial," Eleanor later wrote.

Allenswood headmistress Marie Souvestre said that Eleanor was not only smart, but also had "the warmest heart that I have ever encountered."

At age 17, Eleanor made plans to return home. She called her years at Allenswood "the happiest of my life." In fact, she wanted to study at Allenswood for another year. But Grandmother Hall insisted that she come home to make her debut as a lady of marrying age. This debut was called a "coming out" party, and Eleanor would be the center of attention.

Eleanor was well liked by the other students at Allenswood. In this class photo, she is standing in the back row, third from the right.

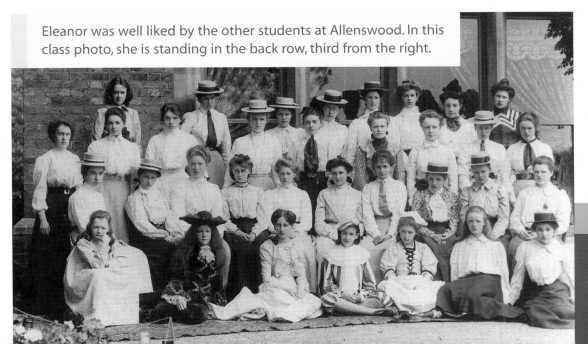

Franklin Roosevelt was a student at Harvard University in Massachusetts when he first started courting Eleanor. In 1903, he asked her to be his wife. Franklin believed Eleanor brought out the best in him.

Back in New York, Eleanor had an unhappy summer at her grandmother's house. The idea of her debut terrified her. She would turn 18 in October and have her coming out that winter. Eleanor once again became uncertain of herself. She felt ashamed that she was not as beautiful as the other young women in her family. She wrote, "There was absolutely nothing about me to attract anybody's attention."

Eleanor was wrong. During a train trip that summer, she happened to see Franklin Roosevelt, a fifth cousin. Franklin quickly took an interest in Eleanor. He saw a stylish, graceful woman with golden hair and sparkling blue eyes. The following winter, Eleanor and Franklin attended many of the same coming out parties and dances. Soon the two began to see each other regularly.

In November 1903, Franklin asked Eleanor to marry him. Eleanor later recalled how surprised she was by his proposal. She asked him, "Why me? I am plain. I have little to bring you." But Franklin disagreed. The young couple was married on March 17, 1905. It wasn't long before Eleanor discovered just how much she could bring to her marriage—and to her country.

Eleanor wore a satin wedding gown covered in lace when she married Franklin in 1905. Her uncle, President Theodore Roosevelt, walked her down the aisle.

The Politician's Wife

After a European honeymoon, Franklin and Eleanor settled into their new life in New York City. Soon they started having children, and Franklin started a successful career. After working as a lawyer, he decided to enter politics. In 1910, he was elected a state senator. The family moved to Albany, New York's state capital. There, Eleanor became a model politician's wife. She entertained guests in their home, met people from many backgrounds, and listened to political debates.

In 1912, President Woodrow Wilson chose Franklin to be Assistant Secretary of the Navy. The Roosevelts moved once again, this time to Washington, D.C. Eleanor went to many political events, and she visited the wives of congressmen and of other important men in politics. Eleanor's support was key to Franklin's political future.

In 1917, the United States was drawn into World War I (1914–1918) in Europe. Franklin readied naval bases, which sent soldiers overseas for the first time. Eleanor worked long hours in

In 1910, Eleanor traveled around New York with Franklin as he campaigned for a seat in the state senate.

The Roosevelts posed for this family photograph in 1916. From left to right, the children are Elliott (born 1910), Franklin Jr. (born 1914), James (born 1907), John (born 1916), and Anna (born 1906). In 1909, another son died from the flu when he was 7 months old.

the local Red Cross canteen. Traveling servicemen stopped there to get a quick meal. Eleanor also knitted wool items to donate to the Navy League. She visited soldiers at the naval hospital. And she helped get more government funds to care for soldiers suffering from mental stress. Eleanor was willing to do any task needed. All her work gave her great satisfaction.

After the war, Eleanor decided to be more independent from her husband. Instead of going to luncheons and tea parties to support her husband's work, she would seek out her own work. Eleanor took classes at a business school. She joined women's groups that worked for peace. In 1920, she joined the

> *"For it isn't enough to talk about peace. One must believe in it. And it isn't enough to believe in it. One must work for it."*
> —Eleanor Roosevelt

League of Women Voters, where she worked to gain equality for women in politics. Eleanor wrote reports for the group on new laws before Congress. Soon she was a key person in the organization. She even gave the first public speech for the group.

Women of the Roaring Twenties

The 1920s were a time of great change in the United States. The fear and gloom of World War I had passed, and people were ready for better times. Businesses were booming and cities were growing. Widespread use of cars, radios, telephones, and electrical appliances gave people more free time. And during this era known as the "Roaring Twenties," women were making great strides in society.

In 1920, Congress approved the 19th Amendment to the Constitution, giving women nationwide the right to vote in elections for the first time. In 1928, women competed in Olympic field events for the first time. That same year, women earned 39 percent of all college degrees, up from 19 percent in 1900. Most people still believed women should stay at home and raise children. But about 20 percent of the work force was women. And instead of being limited to jobs as cooks, dressmakers, and household servants, many women were becoming doctors, lawyers, and bankers.

After winning the right to vote in 1920, these women celebrate their hard-fought victory.

In the summer of 1921, the Roosevelts vacationed on Campobello Island, off the coast of New Brunswick, Canada. That August, Franklin was struck with polio. The disease paralyzed his legs. Franklin learned he would never walk without crutches and would spend most of his time in a wheelchair. Eleanor took care of her husband and wouldn't let him give up his dreams. "Franklin's illness proved a blessing in disguise," Eleanor later wrote, "for it gave him strength and courage he had not had before."

A Political Power

Eleanor (right) and friend Esther Lape hurry to a congressional hearing in Washington, D.C. Eleanor found her political work challenging and fulfilling.

While Franklin focused on regaining his strength, Eleanor focused on politics. She joined the women's division of the New York State Democratic Party and soon rose to be a leader in the organization. She traveled throughout the state to help set up local Democratic clubs for women. And she started writing articles for the *Women's Democratic News*. Eleanor was also a popular speaker at political events and on radio shows. She was becoming a political power.

Eleanor had interests outside of politics, too. She and two friends bought the Todhunter School in New York City, a private school for girls. Eleanor became a teacher at the school. She used the informal style of Mademoiselle Souvestre to teach American history, drama, and literature. Eleanor encouraged her students to think independently and explore new thoughts and ideas. She often told them, "Be somebody; be yourself; be all you can be."

Eleanor (seated at right) poses with a class at Todhunter School, where she worked as a teacher after purchasing the school.

By the late 1920s, Franklin was getting back into politics. His legs were still paralyzed, and he wore leg braces for support when standing. But otherwise he was healthy and ready to get to work. In 1928, Franklin ran for governor of New York and won a close race.

Franklin asked Eleanor to resign her political positions and work for him behind the scenes. He asked Eleanor for her advice, and she traveled with him on trips around the state. Eleanor was often in the public eye, and New Yorkers saw her as someone who cared about them. Eleanor also continued to teach at the Todhunter School a few days a week. "I teach because I love it, I cannot give it up," she said.

"You must do the thing which you think you cannot do."
—Eleanor Roosevelt

Supporters surround Eleanor, Franklin, and their son James to celebrate Franklin's victory in the presidential election of 1932.

During Franklin's first year as governor, the country was in an economic slump. Businesses were closing, and many people were losing their jobs. Then disaster struck on October 29, 1929, when the **stock market** crashed. Many Americans lost their entire savings in a single day. For more than 10 years, the United States was in a period known as the Great Depression. Banks failed. Millions of people were out of work. Families struggled to survive. But Franklin found ways to help the people of New York, and they elected him to a second two-year term as governor.

In 1932, Franklin ran for president. Eleanor threw herself into the work of campaigning, but secretly she did not want to be the First Lady. She didn't want to give up her personal life, her political work, and especially her teaching. On Election Day, Franklin won an easy victory. He would be president of the United States. Eleanor was happy for her husband, but she was uneasy for herself. She later wrote, "The turmoil in my heart and mind was rather great that night." Eleanor wondered what a life as First Lady would bring for her.

Eleanor and the Civil Rights Movement

Eleanor believed the United States could not be a democracy unless all people had the same rights. She saw that blacks did not have the same education and job opportunities as whites. They had poorer housing and often struggled to survive. Whites often found ways to keep blacks from voting. In the South, blacks were segregated—or kept separate—from white people. There were separate schools, churches, restaurants, and even bathrooms for black people and white people.

As First Lady, Eleanor talked to politicians she knew and asked them to work for **civil rights** for blacks. Later, she used her "My Day" column to speak out for civil rights. She joined the board of directors of the National Association for the Advancement of Colored People (NAACP). And in the 1950s, she worked with civil rights leader Martin Luther King Jr. to promote justice and raise money for the civil rights cause.

Eleanor didn't live to see the passage of the Civil Rights Act in 1964. This law states that everyone in America has the same rights. Today, people remember Eleanor for her work to gain equality for all people.

Eleanor meets with leaders of the NAACP, a group that fights for civil rights for blacks.

First Lady of the World

Eleanor waves good-bye as she boards a plane. As First Lady, she crisscrossed the country to learn about the challenges facing Americans.

America had never seen a First Lady like Eleanor Roosevelt. She hosted teas and parties as other First Ladies had. But she also became the first First Lady to have her own career and earn her own money. She wrote articles, had a popular newspaper column called "My Day," appeared on radio shows, and gave speeches. She also held regular press conferences for reporters, something no First Lady had ever done before. Eleanor was changing the role of the First Lady.

Eleanor did all she could to help the nation through the Great Depression. Because Franklin couldn't travel easily, she became his "eyes and ears." She visited poor neighborhoods and worked in soup kitchens, which fed long lines of hungry people. She took a special interest in America's youth, setting up programs to keep children in school and give them healthy meals.

Eleanor visits Camp Tera in New York during the Great Depression. Eleanor sponsored the camp, which provided education and training to jobless young women.

Eleanor flew all around the country, visiting unemployed workers, poor farmers, the hungry, and the homeless. Always on the move, she earned the nickname "Eleanor Everywhere." When she returned home to the White House, Eleanor reported on her travels to Franklin. He respected her opinions and ideas.

Franklin was elected to a second and then a third term as president. A year into his third term, President Roosevelt and the United States faced new challenges. On December 7, 1941, Japan attacked a U.S. naval base at Pearl Harbor, Hawaii. The United States entered World War II (1939–1945) and was soon fighting on two fronts—Europe and the South Pacific. During the war, Eleanor traveled to the South Pacific as a representative of the Red Cross. She greeted U.S. troops, toured army hospitals, and comforted wounded men. Every morning, Eleanor got in the "chow line" for breakfast with the soldiers. Then she took off in a jeep to visit a hospital or to greet soldiers going into battle.

Back in Washington, Franklin continued to be a popular president. He ran for a fourth term in 1944 and won. Before Franklin, no president had ever served more than two terms. But only a few months after his fourth **inauguration**, on April 12, 1945, he died. He did not live to see the end of World War II only four months later, on August 14, 1945.

After her husband's death, many of Eleanor's supporters asked her to run for office. But she refused to be a candidate. She wanted to continue writing about politics and other issues she cared about deeply. But she soon received a phone call from the new president, Harry Truman. He asked Eleanor to serve as one of five U.S. delegates to the United Nations.

On the Home Front

As U.S. soldiers fought World War II in Europe and the South Pacific, life changed for those at home in America. Everyone made sacrifices to support the war effort. Some goods, such as sugar, meat, gas, and tires, were rationed. People could purchase only a small amount. The government needed to ship these goods overseas to soldiers. Even newspapers couldn't use as much paper and printed fewer copies. People also held scrap drives, sold war bonds, and held quilting bees to raise money for the war effort.

   Women stepped in to fill the jobs left behind by soldiers. They became gas station attendants, mail carriers, hospital orderlies, and streetcar conductors. Many women took jobs in factories, making airplane parts and heavy equipment to be used in the war. Women in rural areas grew vegetables in Victory Gardens, canned fruit, and raised chickens to feed their families. Their efforts left more food available to ship overseas for the troops. Women were called "soldiers in housedresses" and "Rosie the Riveter." Their strength at home was important to winning the war.

On the home front, women helped the war effort by planting Victory Gardens (left) and building military equipment, such as this bomber plane (right).

Eleanor talks with John F. Kennedy in 1960. When he became president, Kennedy asked for her help with several projects, including the Peace Corps and his Commission on the Status of Women.

In January 1946, Eleanor traveled to London to attend her first United Nations meeting. She made her mark from the beginning. She gave a speech that convinced the United Nations to allow **refugees** of World War II to live wherever they chose. Members from the Soviet Union had argued that these people should be made to return to their home countries. Later, Eleanor was elected the head of the United Nations Human Rights Commission. One of her greatest accomplishments was the Universal Declaration of Human Rights. Eleanor served in the United Nations until 1953.

At age 68, Eleanor wasn't ready to slow down. She continued to write, teach, and travel around the world. She spoke out against racism and fought for civil rights for blacks. She even started a TV interview show. In 1961, President John F. Kennedy asked her to lead his Commission on the Status of Women. The group studied unfair treatment of women in jobs and society. Eleanor also spent a great deal of time with a loving group of family and friends.

Eleanor became ill with a blood disease and died after a severe stroke on November 7, 1962. She was 78 years old. Americans mourned the loss of a champion for human rights, a woman who had worked hard to improve the lives of people everywhere. At her funeral, former President Truman called Eleanor the "First Lady of the World."

Did You Know?

- Eleanor was known to be an excellent dancer. The Eleanor Roosevelt Reel was named in her honor.

- Eleanor wrote her column "My Day" from late 1935 until her death in 1962. This diary of her public life became one of the most widely read newspaper features in the United States.

- Eleanor was the first president's wife to fly in an airplane.

- All four of Franklin and Eleanor's sons served in World War II.

- Eleanor wrote 27 books, including a three-volume autobiography.

- In 1926, Eleanor and two friends started a small furniture factory called Val-Kill Industries in Hyde Park, New York.

- Many causes that Eleanor worked for were controversial. For this reason, the FBI kept a large file on her activities.

- In 1998, President Bill Clinton established the Eleanor Roosevelt Human Rights Award, given to those who lead the fight for human rights in the United States and around the world.

Eleanor celebrates her 76th birthday on October 11, 1960. Toward the end of her life, she noted there were "few challenges that I am not willing to face."

For most of the years that Eleanor wrote her "My Day" column, the feature appeared six days a week in about 180 newspapers.

My Day By ELEANOR ROOSEVELT

Las Vegas.

A dealer in hearing aids in Cedar Falls, Iowa, says that, because I recommend a certain hearing aid, many people whom he could fit with something that suits them better refuse to accept it. So I want to explain to one and all that, for me, this hearing aid has filled my needs in a remarkable way.

I use it primarily at the theater, in public meetings and in board meetings and in conversations with small groups of people. It makes all the difference in the ease with which I hear because it magnifies sound.

But no one should take a hearing aid without consulting with his doctor or discussing carefully the conditions for which he needs help. One thing may well suit one person and another thing another person.

I certainly would not want people to take my advice blindly merely because I have found the greatest help with a certain make of hearing aid that is so conveniently placed in my eyeglasses.

I am grateful to the gentleman from Iowa for drawing this situation to my attention. It had never occurred to me that people would do more than try something that I had found good, naturally bearing in mind that their needs might be different and would be concerned only with what best suits their needs.

* * *

I appeared at a hearing during the week on the proposed changes in New York's Washington Square, which I hope very much will remain just as it is.

It does not seem to me important that Fifth Av. be extended below where it now begins. What does seem important is preserving the peace and quiet

of the square, for we have few places of that kind in the city.

A city as big as ours develops neighborhoods, each with its own personality, and these neighborhoods contribute to the character of the whole city. Greenwich Village and Washington Square are a real neighborhood and we should do nothing to change their character.

I am even sorry it was not possible to preserve some of the old and historically interesting houses on the north side of the square, but the development on the south side of the square seems to have added to the area's peace and calm. The fact that it is a quiet spot for the students of New York University, for the children and old people who sit on the benches, gives it particular character.

Our passion for destroying and rebuilding everywhere should be curtailed somewhat so that we do preserve a few spots that remain more or less the same and can be revisited and evoke past history.

I have always liked to walk down some of the streets surrounding the square and remember the stories that an old lady, a cousin of mine named Mrs. Weekes, told me when she came to that neighborhood. Her husband did not think it proper for her to go out alone and carry her market basket, so he carried the basket and clung to his arm while they purchased the household needs for the day. This same old lady had danced with Lafayette!

NEW YORK POST, SUNDAY, MAY 18, 1958   M 7

Important Dates

October 11, 1884: Eleanor is born in New York City.

December 7, 1892: Eleanor's mother dies.

August 14, 1894: Eleanor's father dies. (age 9)

1899–1902: Eleanor attends Allenswood School in England.

March 17, 1905: Eleanor and Franklin marry. (age 20)

1918–1919: Eleanor works with the Red Cross and the Navy Department to help American servicemen during World War I.

1920: Eleanor joins the League of Women Voters; the 19th Amendment is passed, granting women the right to vote. (age 36)

1921: Franklin becomes paralyzed by polio.

1922: Eleanor joins the women's division of the New York State Democratic Party.

1926: Eleanor and two friends purchase the Todhunter School in New York.

October 29, 1929: The stock market crashes.

1932: Franklin is elected president; Eleanor becomes the First Lady. (age 48)

1935: Eleanor starts writing the column "My Day."

December 7, 1941: Japan attacks Pearl Harbor; the United States enters World War II.

1943: Eleanor travels to the South Pacific to visit soldiers.

April 12, 1945: Franklin dies. (age 60)

1946: Eleanor attends her first meeting as a U.S. delegate to the United Nations; she is elected head of the Human Rights Commission.

1948: The United Nations passes the Universal Declaration of Human Rights.

1961: President John F. Kennedy asks Eleanor to lead his Commission on the Status of Women.

November 7, 1962: Eleanor dies in New York City. (age 78)

Marian Anderson (1897–1993)

Marian Anderson was an opera singer. In 1939, the Daughters of the American Revolution (DAR) would not let her use their auditorium for a concert because she was black. In protest, Eleanor resigned from the DAR. Later, Anderson became the first African American to be a permanent member of the Metropolitan Opera in New York City.

Amelia Earhart (1897–1937)

Amelia Earhart was the first woman pilot to fly solo across the Atlantic Ocean. When Eleanor was the First Lady, Earhart once flew her from Washington, D.C., to Baltimore, Maryland. In 1937, Earhart attempted to fly around the world. But she was killed when her plane went down.

Mary A. Hallaren (1907–)

Mary A. Hallaren is considered one of the "giants among military women." In 1942, Hallaren enlisted in the Women's Auxiliary Army Corps (WAACS). This army branch later became known as the Women's Army Corps. Hallaren commanded the first battalion of the WAACS during World War II. She secured the permanent presence of women in the military.

Dorothea Lange (1895–1965)

Dorothea Lange was a photographer. During the Great Depression, she took powerful images that showed the hard times people were going through. She photographed people standing in bread lines, migrant workers, and struggling farmers. Lange's images appeared in newspapers around the country.

Jeannette Rankin (1880–1973)

In 1917, Jeannette Rankin became the first woman to serve in the U.S. Congress. She served a second term from 1941 to 1943. Like Eleanor Roosevelt, Rankin worked for peace among nations. She was the only member of Congress to vote against the United States entering World War II.

Glossary

alcoholic (al-kuh-HAWL-ik) someone who has a disease called alcoholism; alcoholics cannot stop drinking alcohol—such as wine, beer, or whiskey—even when it hurts their body, mind, or abilities.

civil rights (SIV-uhl RITES) the rights that a country's citizens have by law; in the United States, civil rights often mean the rights described in the Constitution, such as freedom of speech, freedom of religion, and equal protection under the law.

delegate (DEL-uh-guht) someone who represents other people at a meeting

humanitarian (hyoo-man-uh-TAYR-ee-uhn) someone who works to relieve the suffering of others and make their lives better

inauguration (in-aw-gyuh-RAY-shun) a ceremony in which someone is sworn into government office

politics (POL-uh-tiks) the actions and discussions involved in governing a country; also the activities of politicians and political parties

racism (RAYS-ihz-uhm) the belief that a person's race decides what a person's character is and what he or she can achieve; also the belief that one race of people is better than another

refugee (ref-yoo-JEE) a person who is forced to leave his or her country because of war, disaster, or unfair treatment

stock market (STAHCK MAR-ket) the place where people buy and sell stocks and bonds; stocks and bonds are sold in shares, which each stand for a piece of ownership in a company.

United Nations (yoo-NITE-uhd NAY-shuns) an organization made up of countries around the world; delegates from member-countries work together to maintain peace in the world and solve international problems.

READ THESE BOOKS

Nonfiction

Cohen, Robert, ed. *Dear Mrs. Roosevelt: Letters from Children of the Great Depression.* Chapel Hill: University of North Carolina Press, 2002.

Panchyk, Richard. *World War II for Kids: A History with 21 Activities.* Chicago: Chicago Review Press, 2002.

Parks, Deborah A. and Melva L. Ware. *Eleanor Roosevelt: Freedom's Champion.* Alexandria, Va.: Time Life Education, 1999.

Winget, Mary. *Eleanor Roosevelt.* Minneapolis: Lerner Publications Company, 2003.

Fiction

De Young, C. Coco. *A Letter to Mrs. Roosevelt.* New York: Delacorte Press, 1999.

Zeinert, Karen. *To Touch the Stars: A Story of World War II.* Lincolnwood, Ill.: Jamestown Education, 2000.

LOOK UP THESE INTERNET SITES

The American Experience: Eleanor Roosevelt

www.pbs.org/wgbh/amex/eleanor

View a time line of Eleanor's life, read some of her "My Day" columns, see the Roosevelt family tree, and follow her South Pacific tour during World War II.

Dear Mrs. Roosevelt

newdeal.feri.org/eleanor

Learn more about the Great Depression and read letters Eleanor received from children.

Franklin D. Roosevelt Presidential Library and Museum

www.fdrlibrary.marist.edu/educat33.html

This site features biographies and family photographs of Franklin and Eleanor.

United Nations: CyberSchoolbus

www.un.org/Pubs/CyberSchoolBus/index.html

This site for students offers information about human rights and other issues addressed by the United Nations.

Internet search key words:
Eleanor Roosevelt, Franklin Roosevelt, Roaring Twenties, Great Depression, World War II, Civil Rights Movement, Human Rights

Index